"**The first edition** of the book, released in 2009, transformed the way many agencies around the world look at the creative brief. It's the reason it's #1 on the Advertising Channel's must read list. Now, Howard Ibach has expanded on the original text, resulting in a book that is a must read for every advertising professional working today. On behalf every creative working in advertising today, thank you Howard Ibach. This is a book no one wanted to write, but everyone wanted to read."

— Paul Suggett
Advertising Expert, About.com
Aurora, CO

"**If you are like me**, you have been guilty of writing a novel as a creative brief. The excuse always given, 'There is just too much information that must be included' but as the brief writer it is your responsibility to filter the information down to just the most important nuggets of information. What this book really does well is show you examples of really good creative briefs and explains in detail what each section is supposed to do."

— Jonathan Chiriboga
Marketer, strategist, speaker and social media junkie
Toronto, Ontario

"**There's a tendency** when setting out to create great ads to look at other ads and try to emulate them. Wrong. Wrong. Wrong. Howard's book hits the nail on the head, and suggests instead we start where all great ads (which is to say, non scam and great) do: with a great brief.

"The advice it gives is excellent; the examples some of the best you'll find and the writing style clear and compelling."

— Vaughn Davis
    Owner and Creative Director, The Goat Farm Ltd
    Auckland, New Zealand

"**Why didn't someone show me** this before I had to write my first briefs? I didn't have a clue. But I did have a template, and something my boss had written for Coldwell Banker. Ha! (Howard) nailed that."

— Tom Lehr, President & CEO, Dailey
    West Hollywood, CA

"...**(Y)ou can't do much better** than to dog-ear this book from cover to cover and back again. Step-by-step, chapter by chapter, illustration by illustration (yes, there are pictures, too), Howard not only builds his case for how absolutely indispensable an inspired creative brief is but then proceeds to teach you exactly how to do it: simply, clearly and logically. Making generous use of productive exercises, memorable examples, fascinating case histories, plus the words and deeds of some of the smartest and most insightful people in the field.

"All of the above in a charming, personable, tongue-in-cheek style that makes *How to Write an Inspired Creative Brief* not only a pleasure to read, but a well-nigh essential foundation on which to build a successful advertising career."

— Dave Butler, Creative Director (retired)
    TBWA/Chiat/Day
    Los Angeles

How To Write An

Inspired
Creative
Brief.

2nd edition

By Howard Ibach

Published by:

Juju Books
Austin, Texas

ISBN: 978-0-692-42576-3

Printed in the United States of America

1st edition, August 2009
2nd edition, July 2015

Author photo credit:
Sandra Simon
www.graphoart.com

Design by Rubin Cordaro Design

For Chioma

Table of Contents

Introduction to the second edition

I have learned many things since writing this book, but perhaps the most remarkable is this: Trust your instincts.

The creative brief may be the least sexy aspect of the creative process, but it is without doubt the most important. I was convinced that a book that dissected, and explained how to write, a creative brief was long overdue. It turns out I was right.

What began as a workbook for a day-long workshop that I launched in 2008, which remains an in-demand and growing business that allows me to travel across the country meeting and conversing with industry professionals, evolved into what is now the second edition with a new introduction, and new and expanded chapters. The book, published originally in 2009, continues to sell and receive accolades from advertising, marketing and PR practitioners all across the globe. I am both astonished at its reception and grateful.

In this new edition, I have expanded the text in four areas: The single-minded proposition; collaborating in writing the brief; applying the "Deep Target Dive," an effective self-guided technique to discover consumer insights when a research budget isn't available; and how to tell the difference between well-written and poorly written briefs.

The result is 30% more content in a graphic textbook designed for acolytes and veterans alike. (Seasoned brief writers may scoff, but remember: The best athletes in the world remain on top by returning to fundamentals.) Use the exercises in this book to hone your muscle memory. This will pay off as you become a more experienced brief writer and, one hopes, a respected teacher of brief writing where you work.

I know there are many inspired creative briefs out there. I have seen them. The problem is getting my hands on them. So I ask for your help: Please send me a sample of what you think is a killer brief. You don't have to send a complete brief. If you believe one or more boxes in a brief you wrote or worked from is especially inspired, send those parts to me. I will use the best of the best for the next edition. I may also use them in my workshop, and perhaps publish one or more on my blog. Rest assured, you will receive credit for the work. Visit www.howardibach.com and use the "Contact" page to reach me. If I decide to publish your brief, I'll contact you.

In my travels and discussions, I've discovered my initial instinct, that the creative brief is the poor stepchild of the creative process, remains intact, regrettably. It gets little or no respect. Its ubiquity creates contempt, and we take the document for granted. That is a grand mistake and we have no one to blame but ourselves. This new edition attempts, once again, to slap us out of our collective malaise.

Creative brief writers of the world, unite! We have nothing to lose but our complacency.

Howard Ibach
Los Angeles

Introduction

In my experience, the creative brief is the Rodney Dangerfield of business documents in the world of professional communications. It gets no respect. Not because it isn't used. It is.

The respect thing arises because the creative brief is so ubiquitous that it's taken for granted. It's part of the scenery and no one really sees it for its true value.

It's our own fault, too. Those of us in communications have short attention spans and get bored easily. We're the original A.D.D. sufferers. We'd rather spruce up the creative-brief template than work on filling in the boxes with better answers.

I wrote this book to show you that anyone can write an inspired creative brief. There's an inner visionary you just haven't discovered yet, and I'm here to show you the way.

This book is for anyone who:
- Sells a product or service
- Works with marketing, advertising, PR, interactive or web-based professionals
- Is an advertising, marketing, PR, interactive or web-based account manager, executive, supervisor or director and either writes or directs those who write creative briefs for creative teams
- Is an advertising, marketing, PR, interactive or web-based creative (i.e. writer or art director) who works from the creative brief to produce any form of communication for a product or service
- Is an educator who teaches marketing, advertising or PR
- Is a student of business, marketing, advertising or PR

This book is a companion to a workshop I authored and facilitate, *Inspired Creative Brief Workshop*, which is designed to engage participants with individual and group exercises, and includes a multimedia presentation. But this book is still a teaching device and therefore interactive. You'll find a few exercises and teasers sprinkled throughout.

And it's the result of a lot of reading and working from creative briefs in 20+ years in the advertising agency and marketing services businesses. I've seen every kind of brief, from the mediocre to a piece of literature. Few of the latter, many of the former.

The book exists because I could find nothing like it anywhere, in the library or online. It's not the final word I'm sure. I hope it sparks interest and discussion.

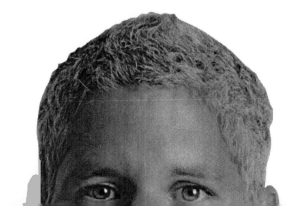

"**Rules**
inspire
creativity."

1 Build a better box.

When I began my career as a copywriter, I viewed rules with disdain. I wanted nothing to interfere with the creative process. Nothing to stand between me and a big idea. You know, the whole "live free or die" thing. It's a philosophy the young and inexperienced find especially appealing.

Now, 30 years into my career, I have a different view.

It's not that I've become a conformist. Hardly. It's that I understand the liberating nature of constraint. The tighter the box in which you force me to work, the more likely it is that I'll find a way to produce a big idea.

I was reading an article somewhere, I no longer remember the publication, when I came across the following three words:

Rules inspire creativity.

They got me thinking about the creative brief. Because the brief is a document filled with rules. You might even say constraints. These constraints are imposed on the brief writer for a reason. The brief is designed to be an act of *reduction*, of summarizing as succinctly as possible, the very essence of a product or service's most desirable attributes.

You, the creative brief writer, are forcing your creative team to live inside a box. The size of that box, big or small, is in your hands. No matter how you look at it, you're a box builder. You're creating rules for the creatives to follow (and, one hopes, about which they feel liberated not constrained).

So why not approach the task with the sense of possibility?

To write an inspired creative brief requires you to bring creativity to the task. It requires you to dig a little deeper, research a little more, ask pertinent questions (maybe even impertinent questions now and then). In short, to write an inspired brief requires the same things of a brief writer that creatives need to produce great work.

Rules may seem like speed bumps, but only to the uninitiated and inexperienced. The challenge of identifying to whom you are addressing the communications can either be phoned in, and the result is a list of bullet points that mean nothing. Or you can be inspired and create a persona, a word-picture of Mr. or Mrs. or Ms. Brand User with the same attention to detail as a short-story writer or poet (more on this up ahead). It's up to you.

You can cut and paste the client's suggestion for the key message and let the creatives figure it out. Or you can put your mark on the project from the beginning.

Creatives, the really good ones that is, use rules to help them. To inspire them. To liberate them from perceived constraints.

Brief writers have the same opportunity. You can let the apparent constraints of a brief template smother your creativity. Or inspire it.

I think you know which option I recommend.

"Do not pass **Go**. Do not collect **$200**."

2 Strategy first, creative brief second.

A simple, clear word of warning:

IF YOU DO NOT HAVE A STRATEGY, YOU CANNOT WRITE A CREATIVE BRIEF.

The creative brief is the first step of the creative process. It's not part of the strategic process.

The strategic process is where you develop the, you know, strategy.

So, no strategy on your creative brief?

Speak up.
Complain.

Then take an early lunch.

13

"When all else fails, **read** the directions."

3 Five reasons why you don't need a creative brief. (uh-huh...)

With tongue planted firmly in cheek, this is my way of introducing you to some real world attitudes toward the document we call the creative brief. I'm not making this up. I've heard these reasons spoken out loud by real, flesh-and-blood, breathing people who claimed to be alive.

BROUGHT TO YOU BY THE DEPARTMENT OF REDUNDANCY DEPARTMENT

"The creative team is brilliant. They'll figure it out."

Maybe. If you're lucky.

But experience tells me that very few people can just "figure out" a creative brief that inspires the desired results.

And even if you are lucky, that's still no guarantee.

Your creative team may be very good at what they do in terms of creative ideas that sell. But passing the buck on the creative brief sets you up for problems, including wasted time and money.

"Everyone knows what we want to do."

Yeah, your people are all clairvoyant, too.

Your company consists of good people and they'll have disagreements. You'll discover this as soon as you write a draft of a creative brief.

The time to learn about those disagreements is before you assign the project. Not after the ideas get presented and someone says, "Yeah, but we never show photos of club members with their shirts off. Didn't someone tell you that?" (This actually happened to me when I presented work to a client in the health club business that showed a chiseled bodybuilder sans t-shirt. Nowhere in the brief was this little tidbit mentioned, and it could have saved everyone the embarrassment.)

17

"We don't do anything briefly around here."

You must be the people with the thousand-page Website.

Brief doesn't necessarily mean fewest words possible. Some well-written briefs can be five pages.

As a wise creative director once said, "Give me the freedom of a tightly written creative brief."

"We always just have a meeting and everyone takes good notes."

When was the last time you played that child's game called "Telephone"? I rest my case.

1

"The deadline is yesterday."

Ah, yes. You have no time to write a creative brief.

I saw a poster in the office of a print production colleague that reads, "Lack of planning on your part doesn't constitute an emergency on my part."

I also remembered this one: "There's never time to do it right, but there's always time to do it over."

When you operate without a creative brief, you're flying by the seat of your pants. Worse, you're flying blind. That translates into wasted time, wasted money, wasted opportunities.

19

"Imitation is the sincerest form of flattery."

4 The education of a creative-brief writer.

If part of your job is writing creative briefs, allow me to ask you a question point blank:

Where did you learn how?

Be honest.

I'm willing to bet that unless you're an account planner, a very specialized title that requires specialized training, you learned to write a creative brief *by doing*. Or more accurately *by copying*. You looked at a creative brief written by someone else, your supervisor or maybe a colleague who'd been on the job a little longer than you, and did as she did.

Hey, it's one way to learn.

But you're reading this book because—and here I'm taking a leap of faith—you think it's far from the ideal way to learn.

And unless you live in Canada or the UK, there are very few places that will teach you the art of writing creative briefs. I know. I checked.

Okay, a bit of truth in advertising: I *am not* an account planner. I'm a copywriter who reads creative briefs almost everyday.

For the purposes of this publication, you're the target of my lecture, the object of my obsession.

You're also the colleague I believe is more than capable of writing stellar briefs.

That's what this book is about: A guide to help you hone your skills, skills you may not realize you already possess. Writing an inspired creative brief is not about rocket science.

K.I.S.S. If you know this one (Keep It Simple, Stupid) you already know the essentials of writing a brilliant creative brief. See, I told you it's not rocket science.

I *am not* an account planner.

"You don't eat the **sizzle**, you eat the **steak**."

5 This book is not about the creative brief template.

Let's get one thing clear before I dive in:

This book is not about writing or creating a creative-brief *template*. I may be going out on a limb here, but I will assume that you already have one of those.

In fact, I'll go even further and say that tucked away in some dark, dusty corner, your company, agency or department has a file cabinet, or more likely a file folder on a server, inside of which is an assortment of creative-brief templates dating back to the last millennium. They all have this label: The new and improved creative-brief template!

The folder gets fatter each year as the last version is laid to rest. Forever.

The creative-brief template is just like Giorgio Armani's closet. You want to believe he designed this very personal space to be an elegant, warm, inviting sanctuary for his wardrobe. Even empty it would be cool to see.

But it's the clothes, stupid! You want to know what he hangs up there!

That's the difference between a creative-brief template and the creative brief you write.

Anyone can fashion (no pun intended) a thoughtful template, even a clever and provocative template. That's the easy part.

The hard part comes when you try to fill in the blanks with inspiring, insightful, relevant information that creatives can use to produce compelling advertising.

There's a lot of talk about this agency or that saying it wants to revise its creative brief, that it's not working hard enough. About planners who believe no two creative briefs should look the same. Each project demands its own brief. Different creative disciplines, in fact, require different templates.

All valid points. I've always believed that the brief should be an organic document that can adapt and change.

Just remember this central truth:

Content rules.

As Giorgio might say, everything else is an accessory.

I'll have suggestions about a template, of course. But my suggestions are meant to show that the template can and probably must adapt according to circumstances.

"You talkin' to

me?"

— Travis Bickle from *Taxi Driver*

Remember who you're writing the brief for: the creative team.

For purposes of discussion the "creative team" refers to a creative director, copywriter, art director or designer. In short, anyone at the client, the ad agency or part of a creative freelance team who's responsible for creating communications for the product or service.

That covers a lot of territory, which is why I'll use the generic "creative" in this book.

Rule of thumb: Creatives are just like other people, except that they're different.

In an article for *Admap Magazine*, David Barker writes that creative people are:

> "...insecure, frustrated, inner driven, stubborn, protective, follow instinct not logic, trust only themselves, love fame, are driven by their own standards and esteem, dismissive of others' opinions, irascible about criticism and often bad editors of their own work."

Then he adds:

> "Creatives live with fear the terror of the blank space. But there's a lot you, as supplier of the brief, can do about that."

Indeed you can.

Continue by taking these observations to heart:

Talk to your creatives before you write a creative brief. They don't work alone. Why should you?

Always take a point of view when you write the brief.

Remember that the creative brief is a contract between you and your creative team.

That's why it's so important to make the brief inspiring. If you succeed in doing that, someone very important will remember who wrote the brief: You.

Attach a copy to your resumé so you can show it off.

"For every
complex problem,
there is a
solution that is

simple, neat
and wrong."

— H. L. Mencken

7 Who gets to write the first ad?

If writing this thing called the creative brief were truly an easy exercise, your 97-year-old grandmother would be doing it. Or your five-year-old nephew.

Well, the creative brief isn't easy. It's not meant to be easy. And it shouldn't be easy.

But it can and must be *easier*.

So here's a great analogy:

The creative brief is a print ad that offers the first creative thinking for the copywriter and the art director.

This idea comes from a book entitled *Truth, Lies and Advertising: The Art of Account Planning* by Jon Steel.

Here's an excerpt:

> "I once heard a planner ask John Hegarty, the creative director of the top London agency Bartle Bogle Hegarty, what he looked for in a creative brief. He replied that he looked for a very simple, single-minded idea, which is usually expressed in the part of the brief that many agencies term the *proposition*. Hegarty said that it was his habit to take that one sentence and write it on a large piece of paper, above or below a picture

The Creative Brief

It's impo... ...say
~~what~~ wh... ...n
important... ...d
who yo... ...nce
is. This ad... ...ed
to talk di... ...th the
peop... ...
a...

of the product, almost as if the line from the brief were a headline. Then he would pin it up above his desk and ask himself first whether the juxtaposition of that line and that product made some rational sense, and second, whether it also started to suggest something interesting on an emotional level. If so, then he would think, *'There's the first ad in the campaign. It's my job to create something better.'"* (emphasis added)

I share this sage piece of advice not to intimidate, although it's a weighty thought, but rather to liberate and enlighten.

Writing a creative brief is not rocket science (I know I said that earlier. Get used to it because I'll say it again. And again). Brief writers know more than they think they know, which is why it's so disappointing to work from briefs that appear to have been written five minutes before they came off the printer.

I also like to point out that writing the creative brief is your opportunity to influence in a very positive way the creative outcome of the project. It's your chance to drive that outcome.

Jon Steel adds this challenge on the next page of his book:

"If the writer of the brief finds it impossible to manifest his or her own thinking in an advertising idea, then it will likely be an uphill struggle for the team assigned to create the actual campaign.

"A brief tends to succeed in direct proportion to the level of creativity present in both its idea and presentation. If the creative brief is not itself creative, if it does not suggest solutions to problems, present information in an expansive and interesting way, and interpret that information with imagination and flair, *then its authors and presenters have no right to expect anything different from their creative teams.*" (emphasis added)

Don't panic:

your "creative brief as ad" doesn't have to be a great ad. It doesn't even have to be good. But as Jon Steel quotes Hegarty, "...it does have to be interesting on both a rational and emotional level."

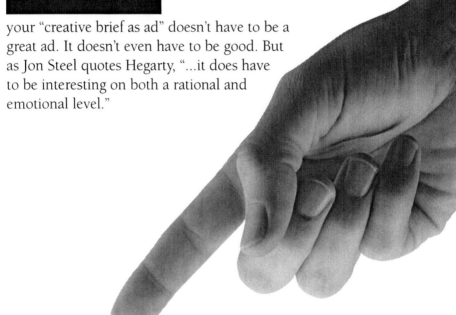

Keep this in mind:

You'll write a better brief if you don't do it by yourself. Collaborate with your creative team. Ask them for their ideas. They have a stake in it.

That's how you'll write a better "first ad" for your creative team.

"Gettin' good players is **easy**. Gettin' 'em to **play together** is the **hard part**."

— Casey Stengel

8 Never write a creative brief by yourself.

Never. Never. Never.

Always collaborate: With another

brief writer. With someone on the creative team who'll be working from your brief. With your boss. I am *not* suggesting a committee. I *am* suggesting a team.

Remember: creatives *always* work in teams. They produce better work that way. Why would it be any different in writing a creative brief?

Account planners have their own thoughts on this subject, and from what I've read many are acknowledging the need to deemphasize the silo-ed nature of job responsibilities and are moving toward a team-oriented, collaborative process when it comes to writing a creative brief.

By "silo" I mean that the account planner writes the brief, delivers it to the account management team who then, in tandem with the planner, briefs the creative team. Three separate job responsibilities with nary a word spoken between them before the dramatic *creative briefing*, which often takes place in some special conference room reserved for big meetings.

It's still done this way at many agencies. Thankfully, this practice is going the way of the…fill in the blank with your favorite antiquated practice. The point is, it's going away.

This change reflects the constantly evolving state of things in the ad world, and the nature of how advertisers talk to consumers. So whether you work at an ad agency, a company that hires ad agencies or you're a creative who works in one or the other environment,

I'm talking to you.

Anything you can do to build trust between the parties involved with the creative process on the agency side and the client side reaps tons of benefits for everyone.

Typically, an advertiser will deliver to its ad agency what's called a Client Brief. This is the document created by the client outlining the *problem* it's asking the ad agency to solve.

The ad agency, in turn, writes its Creative Brief. Think of it as a kind of "call and response" technique. The Client Brief states the *problem* (call) and the Creative Brief addresses the *solution* (response). Clearly the content of the Creative Brief will be different from the Client Brief.

And it's at this intersection where collaboration presents the most ripe opportunity. Collaboration not merely between all the players on the ad agency side (planners, account management and creative, which is a good thing all by itself) but between the ad agency and the advertiser.

Contrary to those who might think this kind of partnership diminishes the unique creative "problem solver" position the ad agency believes it must own to sustain its raison d'etre, I believe the collaborative partnering strengthens this position.

According to a paper published in June 2009 by the World Advertising Research Center (WARC) in London by Nick Southgate entitled, "Three key steps to creative briefing," part of its WARC Best Practice series, all parties acknowledge this development.

Writes Mr. Southgate:

"More and more, both clients and agencies are looking to harness these alternative sources of creativity and put them to work in a creative briefing that is collaborative and collective, rather than linear and sequential."

So what does this mean for you? If you're involved in writing the creative brief, begin by inviting others to the task and make it a team effort. Creative briefs are difficult documents to write, and doing it solo is cruel and unusual punishment.

Instead, develop a unique process around your creative brief where the writing of it in a collaborative setting produces not just a good brief, but an inspired brief. A brief that leads to better creative, more effective creative, creative that produces better results, better sales, and more profits.

As David Ogilvy used to say:

"IF IT DOESN'T SELL, IT'S NOT CREATIVE."

If the creative brief isn't creative (or inspired, or inspiring), it won't produce creative that sells.

And that's why collaborating on writing a creative brief is so important.

"When in

Rome..."

9 The lingua franca of creative briefs: A common vocabulary.

I'm a huge fan of Kevin Costner. A few years ago he made a film called *The Guardian*, a fun action romp that also happens to pay tribute to Coast Guard rescue swimmers.

I was watching the film again recently when a scene about Coast Guard training produced an epiphany.

A senior Coast Guard officer was addressing younger Coast Guard officers about his experiences in the aftermath of Hurricane Katrina. What he said struck me as a solution to a problem faced by creative brief writers.

In the movie, the actor playing the Coast Guard officer said that the training he received as a cadet was the same as every other cadet. So no matter where he was assigned and no matter with whom, he knew he could trust his fellow officers to do their jobs and do them well.

Everyone received the same training.

This is the idea that serves as the foundation of my workshop on writing inspired creative briefs. And for this book.

What creative brief writers need most and don't have is:

A common vocabulary

In other words, call it the creative brief writer's version of what every U.S. Coast Guard cadet receives at Basic Training.

What do I mean by a common vocabulary?

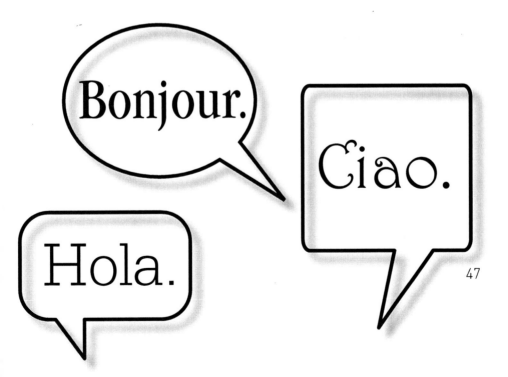

Generally speaking, all briefs ask a series of questions designed to help the creative team understand the task they've been assigned. The hope is that the *answers* to those questions provide inspiration for outstanding creative.

Everyone knows what those questions are: Who is our target audience? What are some key insights about this product category? What do we want the target to think? Feel? Do?

But we're all left to scramble when we start writing the answers. The answers, after all, are the heart of the brief. Not the questions.

If every brief writer had at his or her disposal the *same sets of words and phrases* to answer those questions, imagine how much easier the task would become.

Before you gasp in collective horror at the notion of a cookie-cutter, "one-size-fits-all" creative brief, stop and think for a moment.

What is a brief anyway? It's an act of reduction. It's an example of the art of arriving at the essence of a product's unique point of desirability.

If ever there were a document that demands the principle of **K.I.S.S.** (keep it simple stupid), this is it.

Trouble is, far too many creative brief templates look like over-designed ads. They appear to want to show off either their trendiness or their verbosity.

48   I took a creative seminar 25 years ago with the legendary creative director Stavros Cosmopulos. I still love to quote from one of the little booklets he handed out, which I've kept:

"Make your ideas *fancy* and your layouts ROUGH."

It's a notion lost today because we use of computers to make every concept seem like a finished ad.

But it applies to the creative brief.

Forget about the template. Forget about the questions. *Focus on the answers!*

That might seem mind-numbingly obvious until you read a typical creative brief and get pummeled by insider's jargon, inane generalizations and cliches. Everything except useful information.

So the idea of having a common vocabulary starts to look appealing.

Think of it this way: The set of words and phrases I'm talking about do not constitute *the answers* on your creative brief. They are the *building blocks* to an inspired document, the first step in the creative process.

I WILL GIVE YOU EXAMPLES, AND I WILL SHOW YOU HOW TO USE THEM.

Let's get started.

"A **bad beginning** makes a **bad ending**."

— **Euripides**

(Or, "Garbage in, garbage out.")

10 Writing the creative brief is like developing a roll of film.

The creative brief was designed to foster a common vocabulary, to define terms, avoid confusion, and ultimately save time and boat-loads of money.

It's a document around which we can all huddle, call signals and move down the creative field in unison. Okay, that was my first and last sports analogy. But it works, you have to admit. To improve at anything, you need to identify weaknesses and make them better. But you also need to identify strengths and try to make them stronger.

Start by understanding that the creative brief is the *first step* in the creative process. It comes *after* you've figured out the strategy.

Here's a visualization that will help you put the brief in context:

Back in the days before digital cameras, photography buffs used a thing called 35mm film. Do you remember it? It came on a small roll and you had to physically load it into your camera.

52

The hardest part of developing a roll of film is the first step: getting the exposed film onto the take-up reel.

Why?

If you've never done it before, here's what it entails:

First you have to fit the leading piece of the film between a pincer-like holder at the center of the reel. Then you have to spool the film gently onto the take-up reel...

...are you still with me?

No? Not surprising. It's complicated and tedious. And very hard to do.

Really hard, in fact, because of one minor detail I neglected to mention:

You have to do this entire procedure in the dark.

Any exposure to light and the film is ruined.

And here's the main point I'm making:

> **You won't know if you've done it right until the very end, when it's too late to correct any mistakes.**

Which means you have to practice. A lot. Or you risk ruining all those shots you took of your daughter's 2nd birthday party.

That's why writing the creative brief is like developing film.

If you get the brief wrong, the creative work you see at the end of the process, when your team presents it, will also be wrong.

Does this actually happen in the real world?

Yes.
More than people realize.

It happens because briefs are rushed, not well thought out, not well researched or all of the above. It happens because the team never got a brief in the first place so there's no standard against which to measure the creative.

The worst examples of this scenario usually happen when the creative is presented to the client. Everyone is on board, everyone is excited. Until the client speaks up and says, "but that's not what we want to say."

So, writing a creative brief requires *what?*

Remember the old joke:

"How do you get to Carnegie Hall?"

Practice, practice, practice.

Ergo, your first assignment. (I know, this is such a gorgeous book and you don't want to mar it with your chicken scratch, right? We think alike. Use post-it notes if you wish. Or make mental notes. Or get the art director with beautiful handwriting to do the work for you, and start your bonding process.)

What causes the most headaches when you write a creative brief?

1. _____

2. _____

3. _____

4. _____

5. _____

What's the easiest part about writing a creative brief?

1. _____

2. _____

3. _____

4. _____

5. _____

55

Refer back to this exercise as you make your way through the book. If you don't get a satisfactory resolution to all your "headaches" send me an email.

"The **best critique** of a work of art is **another work of art.**"

— Charles Baudelaire

11 What does an inspired creative brief look like?*

It turns out that no two briefs look exactly alike. That's good.

It speaks well for a document that it can be so important and still be adaptable. As I wrote earlier, it's organic, not static. (And it's not rocket science!)

The creative briefs you'll review in this section are, quite simply, well-written and inspired documents. And they're different in one way or another from each other.

But pay close attention to what they have in common. And to the vocabulary used by the writers to answer each section. These examples are from UK agencies. The UK is the birthplace of the art and science of account planning. Many believe that our British cousins are the finest creative-brief writers on the planet. I agree.

It's my job to help correct this imbalance. Beginning with you.

Let's examine each brief for its strengths and, if we can find them, weaknesses.

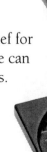

Iceland Range
Creative Brief

What is...
Iceland is a predictable frozen food supermarket that appeals to deal-hunting Mums on a budget

What if...
We revealed some of Iceland's hidden secrets and told Mum about all the other great reasons to shop there?

Why is advertising needed?
Iceland is more than just deals, but you'd never know it with all the deal advertising it does. There is in fact a huge level of product innovation that Mums never know about because they've never been told. Whenever we have researched ideas around their ranges or new products, Mums have always asked (in a rather frustrated way) "why don't they tell us about all these brilliant things?" Iceland now wants to communicate three ranges designed for these budget-conscious busy Mums: Kids Crew, Pizzas and the Christmas lines Party Fayre and Christmas Made Easy.

What is the role for advertising?
This advertising is not just about informing Mums about three ranges, but pitching it in a way that tells them there is more to Iceland than they had ever realised

How do we do this?
By creating an idea or territory that pulls these ranges together and surprises Mum with Iceland's hidden secrets.
This element of 'surprise' or intrusiveness is important as Mums are used to OTT advertising from Iceland and anything too passive, despite how well branded it is, is not usually recalled as Iceland advertising.

Who are we talking to?
Think of the typical, hard-working, under-appreciated Mum trying to feed a demanding family on a tight budget. Iceland is a godsend to them with its amazing deals and the advertising draws them in on a regular basis. However they either go straight for the deals or look for favourites, rarely taking the time to browse and find all the new things Iceland are introducing.
They are family and house proud, live vicariously through celebrity gossip magazines and soaps, have a wide network of sassy Mum-friends (these Mums are surprisingly switched on and 'street smart') and are always looking for something new to make life just a bit easier. Their family is everything, kids especially and it's the needs of the latter that often inform and dictate their needs

Core thought
There's more to Iceland than anyone ever knew

Tone of voice
Enthusiastic, straight-forward and fun

Mandatories
'Because Mums are heroes' endline

This creative brief was written by the folks at a UK agency called hhcl/red cell, which shut its doors in 2007, regrettably. It was a well-known branding agency that won tons of awards and accolades for its creativity. In fact, you may have seen some of its TV spots, particularly for soft drink Black Currant and Maxwell tapes.

59

There are lots of things to love about this brief, and nothing at all to not love.

Start with the opener:

What is…

What if…

As they like to say in the UK, that's brilliant.

What is defines the status quo.

What if is the equivalent of what I'd call communication objectives, which I'll define more clearly in a moment.

So in a typical brief, that question might be posited this way instead:

Reveal some of Iceland's hidden secrets. Inform (tell) Mum about all the other great reasons to shop there.

Either way works fine, but I'm intrigued by the use of a question. Why? Questions get you thinking. Creatives are naturally curious and a question is hard to ignore.

More importantly, notice the use of verbs here, *revealed* and *told*. These are key to writing a clear and inspiring brief. I recommend verbs over adjectives.

Now understand something: I love verbs. They have a need to be doing something. As a writer I have a special affinity for anything that suggests action. I want my reader to do something. To act when she reads my ad.

"Action is character," as F. Scott Fitzgerald said.

60

Use verbs to describe your objectives so creatives get a clear understanding of what the advertising (TV, DM, billboard, banner ad, etc) must accomplish.

Creatives get verbs. Simple, straightforward. They're the John Wayne of words: strong, silent, action-hero types.

Further down in the brief you get to the section *Who are we talking to?* I think this is especially well written. You don't see any bullet points, no acronyms such as HHI. The writer painted a word picture of the typical Mum who shops at Iceland.

Here's another Rule of Thumb: Don't give creatives a list a statistics. Use statistics to create a three-dimensional person, someone real. Create a mini-narrative, a compelling story if you can.

Next is the *core thought*. This is equivalent to the proposition mentioned earlier by John Hegarty. I prefer *single-minded proposition* but they're all synonymous.

is not usually recalled as Iceland advertising.

Who are we talking to?
Think of the typical, hard-working, under-appreciated Mum trying to feed a demanding family on a tight budget. Iceland is a godsend to them with its amazing deals and the advertising draws them in on a regular basis. However they either go straight for the deals or look for favourites, rarely taking the time to browse and find all the new things Iceland are introducing.
They are family and house proud, live vicariously through celebrity gossip magazines and soaps, have a wide network of sassy Mum-friends (these Mums are surprisingly switched on and 'street smart') and are always looking for something new to make life just a bit easier. Their family is everything, kids especially and it's the needs of the latter that often inform and dictate their needs

Core thought
There's more to Iceland than anyone ever knew

Tone of voice

So if I were to write "There's more to Iceland than anyone ever knew" on a piece of paper above or below a photograph of an Iceland supermarket, I'd have to agree with John Hegarty that I held in my hand the first ad for the campaign as outlined on the creative brief.

My job as a copywriter would be to write a better headline.

Finally, I'm very impressed with the brief writer's use of insights under the section called *What are the ranges?* My guess is that *ranges* refers to a product category.

---

hhcl / red cell ··o

What are the ranges?
Kids Crew:
Women's press (assume full page colour) in September to coincide with the start of the new school term

'Surprising' news: A revamped range of kids' food, the hero products of which conform to or exceed Government guidelines on nutrition
Insight: Making it easier for Mum to give good and tasty food to their kids

Pizza range:
Women's press (assume full page colour) in October

'Surprising' news: Iceland have the largest pizza selection on the high street, offering everything from basic pizzas to a new premium pizza line produced in Italy and hand topped with premium ingredients
Insight: The biggest selection of pizzas on the high street (with specific focus on the new premium range)

Christmas range:
:30 TV and Women's press (assume full page colour) in October/December

'Surprising' news: Iceland leads the market when it comes to Christmas food with an extraordinarily wide selection across the Party Fayre line (principally party/buffet food) and the Christmas Made Easy line (everything needed for the Christmas dinner itself)
Insight: Guaranteed to make this Christmas the easiest ever
Note: As this is a Christmas ad we need the requisite level of 'Christmasiness' to give it a festive flavour

---

These insights are like their own propositions, and therefore work as first ads, as if they were headlines.

An even briefer brief comes from glue, a London-based ad agency. The product is called Ello and it's made by Mattel. It's a toy for girls.

This is a tight brief. Very sure footed, no wasted words, to the point.

glue London 31-39 Redchurch Street London E2 7DJ t: 020 7739 2345 f: 020 7920 7801 www.gluelondon.com

Date:	March 2004	Budget:	
Client:	Mattel	Job No:	
Project:	Ello	Team:	

Commercial Context
Ello is a new product launch in the UK for 2003, to be positioned in the Girls Activity area. The girls toy market is highly fragmented. The Girls Activity Market is showing strong growth, of which Mattel want to capture a large share. Girls are already interested in building – 18% of construction toys are bought for girls. It is our aim to help make ello the Market Leader in the Girls Activity Category by developing interactive content to drive interest and raise awareness.

Who are we talking to?
Girls aged 5-10 yrs old. The way they play can be grouped into the following: Budding artists – this child is into crating and drawing. Family Girl: this child is very family orientates, likes games, puzzles and helping out. Collector: this child loves collecting things like stickers, beanies, Barbies etc

What are we trying to achieve?
- To communicate the open ended nature of ello
- To ensure that the child knows and is excited by ello, therefore initiating a request – child desire is at the centre of all toy buying
- To excite girls with a category that is not traditionally girlie. To launch something that is very different for girls – not pink, fluffy, glittery, something that is different from the norm and something that they would not ordinarily choose

Proposition
Endless expression

Why is this true?
Playing and creating with ello is a way for a little girl to truly express herself in a fun way. It is like drawing a picture – it is a statement about herself, her thoughts, her world.

Brand characteristics
Ello is the creation system for girls that inspires them to design and create the most amazing stuff!.. from people to places to jewellery..whatever sparks girls' imaginations!

Media
The microsite will feature on two sites – www.citv.co.uk and www.nick.co.uk

Mandatories
It will need to be fully interactive, so girls can make their own creation on screen with ello. The communication should be in the form of a fully branded microsite, to be hosted on 3rd party websites. We also want to encourage viral activity, so girls should be able to email their creation on to friends. There will be an incentive to forward their creations on e.g. to 5 friends.

Notice first the use of verbs in the section called *What are we trying to achieve?* I gravitate toward verbs a lot, and here's another example:

To communicate…
To ensure…
To excite…and to launch…

Noticing a pattern?

Notice as well that you don't find a laundry list. Four things, very specific.

Next, look at *Proposition*:

Endless expression.

Put that line next to a photo of the product. How would it work as a first ad?

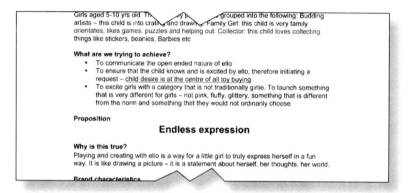

Girls aged 5-10 yrs old. Th[...]y [...] grouped into the following: Budding artists – this child is into cra[...] and draw[...] Family Girl: this child is very family orientates, likes games. puzzles and helping out. Collector: this child loves collecting things like stickers, beanies, Barbies etc

What are we trying to achieve?
• To communicate the open ended nature of ello
• To ensure that the child knows and is excited by ello, therefore initiating a
  request – <u>child desire is at the centre of all toy buying</u>
• To excite girls with a category that is not traditionally girlie. To launch something
  that is very different for girls – not pink, fluffy, glittery. something that is different
  from the norm and something that they would not ordinarily choose

Proposition

Endless expression

Why is this true?
Playing and creating with ello is a way for a little girl to truly express herself in a fun
way. It is like drawing a picture – it is a statement about herself, her thoughts. her world.

Brand characteristics

This brief is part of a PowerPoint presentation that I found on Slide Share. Tango is a popular fruit soft drink in the UK.

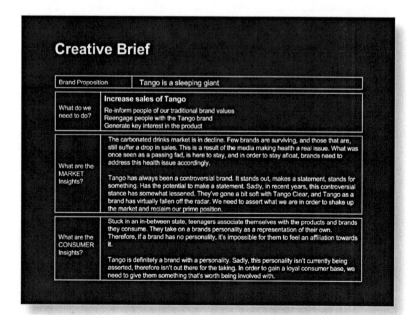

Creative Brief

Brand Proposition	Tango is a sleeping giant
What do we need to do?	**Increase sales of Tango** Re-inform people of our traditional brand values Reengage people with the Tango brand Generate key interest in the product
What are the MARKET Insights?	The carbonated drinks market is in decline. Few brands are surviving, and those that are, still suffer a drop in sales. This is a result of the media making health a real issue. What was once seen as a passing fad, is here to stay, and in order to stay afloat, brands need to address this health issue accordingly. Tango has always been a controversial brand. It stands out, makes a statement, stands for something. Has the potential to make a statement. Sadly, in recent years, this controversial stance has somewhat lessened. They've gone a bit soft with Tango Clear, and Tango as a brand has virtually fallen off the radar. We need to assert what we are in order to shake up the market and reclaim our prime position.
What are the CONSUMER Insights?	Stuck in an in-between state, teenagers associate themselves with the products and brands they consume. They take on a brands personality as a representation of their own. Therefore, if a brand has no personality, it's impossible for them to feel an affiliation towards it. Tango is definitely a brand with a personality. Sadly, this personality isn't currently being asserted, therefore isn't out there for the taking. In order to gain a loyal consumer base, we need to give them something that's worth being involved with.

This is one of the finest, most interesting and well-written creative briefs I've seen in years. Go to school on this document.

My single bone of contention: The first item under *What do we need to do?*

"Increase sales of Tango."

Okay, I'm in favor of clarity as much as the next guy, but c'mon folks. It helps no one in the creative department make an ad when you're told you need to increase sales.

That's a great big "duh."

I actually live for the day when a brief appears before me that reads, "Sales are too high. Create an ad that cools things off."

Now look at the rest of the entries.

What do you see? Verbs:

Re-inform…
Reengage…
Generate…

These statements offer clear instructions to creatives about the task at hand. They get what the advertising has to do.

There's a reason why I keep harping on this. (Keep reading. Slow wind up to the pitch.)

Next, insights! Creatives love insights! If you have them, and this brief is loaded with both market and consumer insights, share!

65

There's no one, universal way to write about insights. It's not like you always use verbs and never nouns and adverbs. When you don't have insights, it's a dilemma. But there are ways around that, which I'll address later in the book.

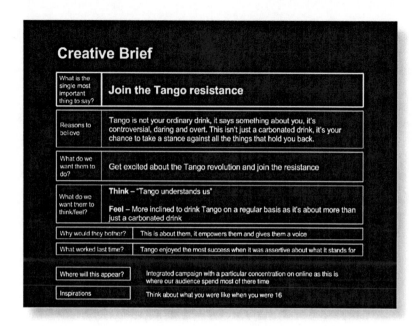

Creative Brief

What is the single most important thing to say?	**Join the Tango resistance**
Reasons to believe	Tango is not your ordinary drink, it says something about you, it's controversial, daring and overt. This isn't just a carbonated drink, it's your chance to take a stance against all the things that hold you back.
What do we want them to do?	Get excited about the Tango revolution and join the resistance
What do we want them to think/feel?	**Think** – "Tango understands us" **Feel** – More inclined to drink Tango on a regular basis as it's about more than just a carbonated drink
Why would they bother?	This is about them, it empowers them and gives them a voice
What worked last time?	Tango enjoyed the most success when it was assertive about what it stands for
Where will this appear?	Integrated campaign with a particular concentration on online as this is where our audience spend most of there time
Inspirations	Think about what you were like when you were 16

What is the single most important thing to say?

Another great variation on single-minded proposition. It works.

And I love the answer:

Join the Tango resistance.

Here, Tango becomes the modifier, the adjective. The key word is *resistance*. And what a great word it is.

The *single* thing is also a great first ad. In fact, it would be a challenge for the creatives to improve on it. And if you've seen the history of Tango's TV spots, the work always shines. Still, this is a great brief. I wish I'd had the chance to work from it.

Finally, the brief writer, a fellow named Vincent Thomé, a French account planner working in London, included creative starters. If you ask me, he's a creative in planner's clothing!

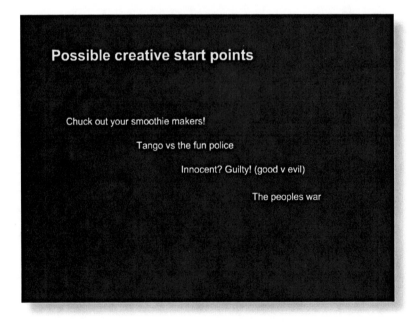

Possible creative start points

Chuck out your smoothie makers!

Tango vs the fun police

Innocent? Guilty! (good v evil)

The peoples war

✱ I am still looking for creative briefs as good as, or better than, the examples I provided here. If you have one, send it to me!

"I'm ready for my

close up

Mr. DeMille."

— Norma Desmond from *Sunset Boulevard*

12 The creative brief is not about the questions. It's about the answers.

Before I start, a quick reminder: I said earlier that I assume you have a creative-brief template already. What follows is simply one version of a template. Adapt the questions to fit your particular circumstances. But I do recommend that each of the following 9 questions be included in one way or another.

Refer to the three UK briefs cited earlier to see how they framed questions.

1. What is the problem we're trying to solve?

Know where you're going before you leave.

Yes, this is obvious. Obvious is also the very thing that gets taken for granted. Or forgotten.

State the problem clearly:

- Sales are down, and we need to acquire new customers
- Sales are down (or flat) and we need to drum up new business from our best customers
- Sales are up, but not as much as we wanted
- We're losing customers because our competition launched a competitive product. We need to respond
- A few negative headlines in the media have hurt our growth, or affected our sales. We need to do something

The problem doesn't have to be a crisis. You could be faced with a good problem: You have a new product or service, and you need to tell the world about it. Call it a challenge if you want. The point is the same. Creatives are problem solvers. The earlier you engage them, the more they can do to help.

But first things first: State the problem or challenge clearly.

Please note that these examples are clearly different than saying "Increase sales." Why? Because these statements, and your variations of them, pinpoint a specific situation. Creatives will solve the problem of "we're losing customers because…" differently than they would if the problem were stated "we need to acquire new customers."

The first is a problem of customer retention, the second is the challenge of customer acquisition. Different challenges, different way into each problem.

2. Why are we communicating?

In other words, what are the objectives?

This particular spot in the creative brief is where confusion rears up and bites people. It's where creatives and account managers start speaking in a different language and are in desperate need of a translator.

Let's ask a fundamental question: What do all communications have in common?

(Answer: They must ask the reader to *do* something, even if it's just to change his or her perception of the product. Ultimately, it should ask the reader to do more than that to be completely effective, such as to call for more information, or go online, or attend an event, or order today! But the point is, a Call to Action is not just for direct-response advertisements!)

Now, what's the difference between business objectives, marketing objectives and communication objectives?

That's not a rhetorical question. It's another quiz.

Define business objectives:

_____

Define marketing objectives:

_____

Define communication objectives:

_____

Which is most relevant to creatives?

_____

Why?

_____

I've seen this question—Why are we communicating?—asked in a variety of ways, including "What do we need to do?", "What are we trying to achieve?", "What if…" followed by a sentence outlining desired outcomes of the creative, and "Why are we advertising?"

It's a simple question. But I've seen it confused with other descriptors such as "marketing objectives" and "business objectives."

They're not the same thing.

The creative brief is written for the creative team, so anything that doesn't discuss what the communications must say and how it's said will be viewed as a tangent, which is my nice way of saying it will be ignored.

That isn't to say that business or marketing objectives are unimportant. They *are* important. Just not to creatives.

Let me put it another way. Business and marketing objectives relate to sales, growing market share, profits, things of that sort. Increasing sales is one thing creatives know their ads have to accomplish, so you won't be telling them anything useful.

Communication objectives are about describing what the advertising has to say, and say well. The best creative briefs I've read over the years address communication objectives by choosing smart, relevant, thought-provoking verbs.

Here are a few examples:

Inspire the consumer to call for a free sample of Brand X
Romance the consumer with Brand R's allure
Re-engage the consumer who's been away from Service T
Excite the consumer about the versatility of Brand K
Convince the consumer that Brand Q will make him
    feel powerful
Educate the consumer about Brand P's superior performance
Remind the consumer that Brand F won taste tests in
    100 cities

You can probably think of dozens of other verbs to do the trick, but the list isn't that long. You need only a few really good verbs, ones you'll use over and over.

The point is, when you use verbs to describe what the advertising must accomplish in the minds and hearts (mostly the hearts) of readers or viewers or listeners, you're giving your creative team clear direction. Pick out three really important things you want the ad to say, no more, and find the right verbs to describe the desired effect.

If you're thinking, "This is what he means by a common vocabulary," pat yourself on the back!

Examples of OBJECTIVES

To CONVINCE
To EDUCATE
To PERSUADE
To REMIND
To REASSURE
To COMPEL
To INFORM
To CONNECT
To ROMANCE
To SEDUCE
To EMPOWER
To ENCOURAGE
To DRIVE
To RE-ENGAGE
To INSTILL
To INSPIRE
To MOTIVATE
To CONVINCE your target to:
   CALL
   JOIN
   BUY
   ATTEND
   BELIEVE
   SUPPORT
   RENEW
   SUBSCRIBE
   CONTRIBUTE

How to uncover core emotional insights about your target audience.

How do people make decisions?

I'm not asking about the sequence of steps someone takes to arrive at a choice between, say, two options when she goes shopping for new jeans.

I'm asking, rhetorically, what part of the brain fires on all cylinders when mulling that range of options?

We know that the right lobe is, in overly simplistic terms, the center of one's emotions.

The left lobe governs reason and language, where analysis takes place.

Given this understanding, which lobe plays the dominant role when our make-believe shopper decides between Levis or Lucky Brand jeans?

The answer to this question, in my opinion, can help you arrive at consumer insights that don't require a research budget.

I'm not a neurologist. I'm an advertising creative. But I know this: we form attachments to a product we like, even love (oops, there's a dead giveaway) by means of our emotional connection to it. If there is no emotional connection, there is no allegiance or loyalty to that product. I've known this to be true for the entire tenure of my advertising career.

75

Thankfully, it's no longer just my opinion.

The Harvard Business Review published a study in 2005 that proved this connection.

To my delight, I found a writer who is asking a similar question, this time in the arena of politics and public policy. *The New York Times* columnist and intellectual David Brooks wrote a piece called "The New Humanism." His premise is remarkably similar to the point I'm making here. I'll quote from his column:

"We have a prevailing view in our society — not only in the policy world, but in many spheres — that we are divided creatures. Reason, which is trustworthy, is separate from the emotions, which are suspect. Society progresses to the extent that reason can suppress the passions.

"This has created a distortion in our culture. We emphasize things that are rational and conscious and are inarticulate about the processes down below. We are really good at talking about material things but bad at talking about emotion."

I found a smile creeping onto my face when I first read David Brooks's column. It seems silly because any of us who practice advertising and brand development understand this relationship intuitively.

Without his saying so, David Brooks seems to suggest that advertising professionals know something about human nature that policy experts don't. Well, then…Lee Clow for president!

We shoot ourselves in the foot when we fail to take seriously our already ingrained understanding of the emotional connection to a product when we prepare to create new advertising for that product.

In other words, we know about the strong play of emotions that helps us decide between Levis and Lucky Brand. Or put another way, when it's time to discard our favorite pair of jeans, that's when we really feel a strong tug on our emotions.

This is precisely what the Deep Target Dive^{SM} is designed to accomplish: Discover and leverage the core emotional benefit of your product or service without spending a dime on research.

When an advertiser fails to pay heed to the emotional core of a brand — because he doesn't trust the acuity of emotion — he's ignoring huge brand equity.

The Harvard Business Review says so. And even a New York Times policy wonk is agreeing.

Here's a trick you can do yourself using what you already know about your target combined with your familiarity with your brand. This technique requires you to hypothesize your customer's unmet needs and unspoken emotional motivations that drive his or her purchase decisions.

The Deep Target Dive^{SM} allows you to wear your "customer" hat and ask a sequence of questions to uncover the key emotional benefit that you can support with rational benefits.

Here's how it works:

First, you have a new client, MetLife. The product you're selling is a one-million dollar life insurance policy. Start here:

What is the feature?

What is the benefit?

(See answer at the back of the book)

1. Now that you've identified the product *benefit*, play the role of the customer and answer, "Why is that important to you?"

2. Continue asking this question until you arrive at a believable emotional motivation for a purchase decision. *You'll have to ask this more than once, and there's no set number of times you repeat the question. You'll know when the emotional motivation is believable. A good test is to go to the point where your answer sounds over the top. Discard that one and what comes **before** should be your core answer.*

MetLife's life insurance policy gives me peace of mind that my loved ones are taken care of if I die.

Why is that important to you?

Because I want my family to know that I'm a good provider. Why is that important to you?

Because it's how I show my family that I love them.

Finish this on your own.

Why is that important to you?

_____

Is this is the key emotional benefit?

_____

Can you keep going? You need only ask "Why is that important to you" a handful of times before you arrive at a credible answer.

4. Who are we talking to?

Draw a picture with words.

A few questions to help you zero in on your core audience. If you have demographics and psychographics, great! If you know enough to create one or more personas, congratulations.

Here are a few key questions every creative wants answers to:

- What percentage of the audience has access to the Web? Email? Cable TV? Mobile device?
- What do we know about the audience's current attitudes toward the brand?
- What objections does the audience have that we need to overcome?
- How will we overcome these objections?
- Can you draw a picture using photos and illustrations of the typical user of the product or service?
- Can you draw a picture of the typical *non*-user of the product or service?

I think the biggest mistake brief writers make when they talk about the target audience is to fill the box with statistics. It's the lazy way to answer this question.

Go back and review the UK briefs and re-read the one for the Iceland Range grocery store. That was an excellent example of a word-picture of the typical Mum who shops at Iceland Range. Not a bullet point anywhere. It's a neat snapshot in the form of a quick narrative.

Here's a shining example from a creative brief written by an especially inspired brief writer from Leo Burnett for a Proctor & Gamble brand you probably know: Vicks.

Who are we talking to?

Cold sufferers. You know how you feel when you've got a cold — that pathetic little inner-child of yours suddenly wakes up and, before you know it, you're moaning & whining, you've gone all whiney & wimpy, all snivel, snot & slovenly; red raw puffy eyes, pale skin, lank hair — everything seems to be sagging! You feel like something from a Salvador Dali painting; you want to snuggle up in bed and dammit — you want your Mummy! But it's not fair, is it, because no one else takes your suffering seriously —"Good God, pull yourself together, man, we're not talking leprosy here! Don't be such a baby, get on with it, stop moaning!"

79

Yes, your instincts tell you to be a child, but you're not allowed to because you've "only" (only!) got a cold. And worse still — oh, the cruel irony! — even your attempts to retain your adulthood in the midst of your suffering betrays that sniveling little inner–child of yours: "oh don't worry about me, I'll be all right...", "...no, no, please, I don't want to sound like a martyr...", "...well, I'm feeling a little better now, thank you..."

I'm sorry, but when you've got a cold you're doomed to be a Child–Adult.

Okay, I admit, this is more, a lot more, than a mere "target audience" box filled in with stats. You get insights into the psyche of someone with a cold (probably you; me, too, because we all act like this when we get a cold, if we can get away with it).

Still, you get my point here, don't you? Isn't this a far more elegant description of someone who might use Vicks than a bunch of stats?

Of course it is.

It's also damn funny! Which makes it equally inspiring. Which means the brief writer pulled out all the stops because he or she knew who was reading it.

Keep this in mind next time you think the box labeled "who are we talking to" is just a box.

It's an invitation. You're invited. No RSVP required.

Write an answer like these examples in your next brief and you'll be honoring your creative team with a truly useful bit of information that will stick to their brain cells.

It's the most important sentence in your creative brief.

Most creatives skip ahead when they read the brief to see what's written in this place. The best SMPs are works of art. Almost headlines in their own right. So succinct, so precise and so finely honed, you almost don't need the rest of the brief.

In fact, the most succinct, precise and finely honed SMPs *are* complete briefs. *Which is why they're so rare.*

They come in many different names:
Unique Selling Proposition
Key Selling Proposition
Key Message
The Elevator Speech
One Memorable Thing

I choose:
Single-minded proposition.

The bed of nails analogy.

Notice the word *single*. It's not the double-minded proposition, or the triple-minded proposition. It's the single-minded proposition.

Meaning ONE THOUGHT.

81

I can't remember how many times I've read a brief with three things listed in the box labeled single-minded proposition.

Why is this concept so important?

Because the best communications are focused. Like a laser. They grab our attention with one killer idea. Not two. Not three.

One.

If you have any doubts, consider the bed of nails analogy. Have you heard about those guys in India who can fall asleep on a bed of nails? (It's true. I'm not making this up.) Well think about it: any communication with lots of points will put the reader to sleep too.

Now imagine a bed with one sharp nail sticking up. Think someone can fall asleep in that bed?

The same is true with any communication. If it has one unforgettable message, like a sharp nail poking the reader, it will be memorable.

Make sure your single-minded proposition is really single minded.

Here is a tip to get you in the right frame of mind:

If you look at the task as if you're writing the "first ad," think about a billboard rather than an ad. Why? Because the best billboards are short. Very short.

Get a copy of a recent *Communication Arts Advertising Annual* or an *Archive* and find examples.

Here's one for the new 2014 Mini Cooper:

Get the picture? Keep your single-minded proposition short, quick, headliney, tagliney.

To help you visualize this short, snappy, headliney single-minded proposition, here's an exercise I like to recommend. It puts you in the mind of the receiver of the ad message, the target audience:

Imagine yourself on one side of Broadway in Times Square just after all the theaters have let out on a Saturday night. Someone who represents your target audience is standing on the other side of Broadway.

In the din and mass of bodies around you, what can you yell (because you're gonna have to yell, right?) that gets your message across?

You can't yell an entire paragraph. You can't yell even a long sentence. Think about that billboard-like line and maybe you could yell that.

Loudly.

That's the effect of a well-written, inspired single-minded proposition.

In fact, if I had to write the brief for a billboard project for the new Mini Cooper, I'd have been delighted to write a single-minded proposition close to or suggesting "Think outside the box" in spite of that phrase's overuse.

That's a hell of a good "first ad." Turns out it's a great billboard.

Here's another technique that works (and I'll continue with the Mini Cooper as our example):

"When I drive the Mini Cooper, I feel..."

Think about a short, billboardy line that you'd yell to your target across a busy Broadway on a Saturday night, then finish that sentence.

You'll end up with a pretty good "first ad" single-minded proposition.

Most of the time, creatives go right to the SMP. So there's a bit of pressure on you, the brief writer, to write something juicy. Hey, that's what you signed up for, right?

But you got it.

Piece of cake.

Short and sweet.

Okay, I'm done.

Where does the Single-Minded Proposition spring from?

No two creative briefs are exactly alike, but most contain a box that asks for "communication objectives" or "reasons why we're creating this advertisement." These two mean the same thing.

A brief also asks for the Single-Minded Proposition (SMP). Sometimes it's called the key proposition or the One Unique Thing. Whatever you call it in your brief, it must list the one overriding reason why people will or should want to buy your product or service.

So where do you find the SMP? In the short list in Communication Objectives. It starts as a product feature for which you, the brief writer, must assign a product benefit (assuming your client hasn't done that already).

From there, the Single-Minded Proposition emerges from the product benefits. A product can have hundreds of benefits, ranging from the core benefit that gives the product its singular appeal, all the way to very tenuous benefits that may in fact be valuable but aren't going to have a significant impact on sales.

86

For example, it's hard to argue with the unique design appeal of an Apple iPad. That's central to its huge popularity. You just want to reach out and hold one. And play with it. That could be the benefit that turns into the SMP.

On the other hand, my favorite chewing gum comes in a sleeve of 12 pieces. Why not 15? Or 9? Is this particular sleeve size a benefit? Well, yeah, but it's not terribly significant. And it won't necessarily effect my purchase decision.

So all product features translate into some kind of product benefit.

They also have the potential to translate into communication objectives, or reasons why we are asked, as creatives, to come up with an ad. However, we're not given a list of eight or nine or 15 communication objectives.

It should be only three, four tops.

But...

The path from product feature to product benefit to Single-Minded Proposition isn't direct. It's not literal.

This spot on the brief is exactly where I think brief writers stumble and over-think things. That's why I'm a big advocate of using a common vocabulary when you write a brief. It's a matter of eliminating confusion and inexactness, and finding the right words to describe what you really mean.

I suggest that you use verbs to write communication objectives. (Review Chapter 12 on page 70)

Why verbs? They're the John Wayne of words. They're about action. About doing something. And we want our targets to do something: Buy the product we're selling.

Let's use Apple again. We know that Apple stands apart in the tablet business because of its clean, intuitive design. I'd argue it's at or near the top of the list of product benefits.

But I wouldn't list "cool design" as a communication objective. It's too vague. It doesn't tell the creative team what to do about this...coolness.

Instead, I'd rather use a verb to guide the creatives in their thinking. I say "guide" rather than "instruct" or "direct" because as a brief writer it's not my job to write the ad. I'm the first step in the creative process.

So, what might I say? Romance...excite...thrill (the verb, not the noun)...energize...

You get the idea, right? Keep it simple. Use direct verbs to describe the reasons why the creative team has been asked to write the ad.

The progression looks like this if we're using the Apple iPad as our example:

Product feature: Uncomplicated, simple design (what the product is)

Product benefit: iPad's cool makes you cool too (what the product gives you)

Remember:
The feature talks to your head.
The benefit talks to your heart.

Communication objective: Jolt the target into falling in love (again) with the latest Apple device (what we want the creative team to do)

Single-Minded Proposition: "_____"
(how to communicate the product benefit that achieves the communication objectives)

(Hey, I know how to do this. You're the one who needs practice. So practice!)

One tip: the SMP can be off the wall and outrageously over the top. How so? *It's not meant for public consumption.* Its purpose is to inspire the creative team. Get their juices flowing. As the brief writer, you get to take the first crack at writing a headline.

So brief writers, arise and be daring. But don't confuse the product benefit with the SMP itself!

Do them in your head.

You can write a brief in three simple steps. It'll take you less then five minutes. Do this once a day, say during your commute to or from work, and you'll discover your brain will add creative-brief-writing muscle before you know it.

Now let's try something harder: the object on which you're sitting right now. A chair.

Step one: identify the features of your chair. As I type this, I'm sitting on a counter stool in my kitchen. My stainless steel and leather stool is comfortable. It's attractive. It was inexpensive. That's three features.

Next, identify what the benefit is for each feature.

Comfort: I gravitate toward this chair because it's comfortable, so I like it. A lot.

Attractive: I feel proud of my excellent taste in design.

Inexpensive: My, aren't I the clever chap for finding something so wonderful and at such a bargain.

Three features, three benefits.

Oh, and guess what. We've already found the hardest thing to write on a creative brief: the Single-Minded Proposition. It's always one of the benefits. Always. The question is, which one?

For your practice exercise, it doesn't matter. Write (in your head) an SMP for *each* benefit. I sometimes provide my creative teams with multiple SMPs. When you did as much creative testing as I did, you often need different creative approaches.

For comfort, try this:

You'd give this chair a standing ovation except you're too comfortable to get up.

For design, try this:

You keep a photograph of this chair in your wallet and show it off any chance you get.

For inexpensive, try this:

If they gave out Nobel Prizes for bargain hunters, you'd get one.

Notice that each SMP could be a headline. They don't have to be good headlines, however. You're the pioneer headline writer on the assignment. Your job is to write the first one to inspire something better from your creative team.

Now, you try it. Pick everyday objects — a pencil, your bedroom slippers, your cereal bowl, a coffee mug, your reading lamp. Keep them simple and unremarkable. It takes the pressure off.

Remember: three features, three benefits, three SMPs.

Also remember John Hegarty's rule that the proposition is the *first ad for the creative team*. So don't be lazy. This is a test.

Be pithy. Be clever. Be succinct.

Before you know it, SMPs will become second nature to you.

Practice writing SMPs.

(This is how copywriters get really good. I'll give you an image, you write an SMP.)

1. The Brooklyn Bridge:

2. Teddy Roosevelt:

3. Your cell phone:

4. Mark Twain:

5. A banana:

Something to think about: *how to practice writing briefs when you don't have time to practice writing briefs.*

Here's how. You can do this anywhere. You can do it any time of day. It doesn't take much time at all. And the more you do it, the better you'll become at writing briefs. Trust me. I do it a lot myself and it works.

I don't know if you can do it in your sleep, but it's worth a try.

Essentially, it's an exercise in writing a single-minded proposition (SMP), which is the most challenging part of the brief. Because if you can write solid, inspired SMPs, you've pretty much written the entire brief. When creatives ask, "What's the brief?" they're really asking, "What's the one thing we need to say?" So you'll end up getting a double creative-brief workout.

Like any exercise you do on your own, only you will know how hard you're trying. Cheat, and you hurt only yourself.

You could begin with an existing client's project, but that's not quite as fun, and to make it fun, take control and pick something you like.

Try this guy, for example.

Anything, animate or not, not only possesses, but deserves, an SMP. Yes, even your mother. Especially your mother.

But start with this familiar face. Ask yourself the same question about George Washington that you'd ask about any other brand. Because he is, after all, kinda well known.

Do you see where I'm going with this? You can practice writing briefs for anything.

Everything has its essence. Its one key thing. Its single-minded proposition. Find that and you've written a creative brief.

So what did you write about George?

6. What's the proof that the SMP is true?

Or, show me the money!

Here's where you list the benefits. Once you've identified your SMP, you have to offer proof that it's believable. Here's where you show off your brand mastery. What are your product's or service's benefits? How do you outshine the competition?

See page 77 and review the differences between a feature and a benefit. Practice again to master your skills! Go ahead...I'll wait.

He who digs deepest uncovers the treasure.

I was introduced to the story that follows very early in my career. It's an old story and perhaps you've read it too.

I've read it in various forms when I did a Google search. Some use it as an illustration of how you figure out a product's single-minded proposition. I think it's a teaching lesson in the value of being intrepid.

It's told by a copywriter named Bud Robbins.

Back in the sixties, I was hired by an ad agency to write copy on the Aeolian Piano Company account. My first assignment was an ad to be placed in *The New York Times* for one of their grand pianos.

The only background information I received was some previous ads, a few faded close-up shots . . . and of course, the due date.

The Account Executive was slightly put out by my request for additional information and his response to my suggestion that I sit down with the client was, "Are you one of those? Can't you just create something? We're up against a closing date!"

I acknowledged his perception that I was one of those, which got us an immediate audience with the head of the agency.

I volunteered that I couldn't even play a piano let alone write about why anyone should spend $5,000 for this piano, especially when they could purchase a Baldwin or Steinway for the same amount.

Both allowed the fact they would gladly resign the Aeolian business for either of the others, however, while waiting for that call, suppose the deadline was attended to.

I persisted and, reluctantly, a tour of the Aeolian factory in upstate New York was arranged. I was assured that "we don't do this with all of our clients" and my knowledge as to the value of company time was greatly reinforced.

The tour of the plant lasted two days and although the care and construction appeared meticulous, $5,000 still seemed to be a lot of money.

Just before leaving, I was escorted into the showroom by the National Sales Manager. In an elegant setting sat their piano alongside the comparably priced Steinway and Baldwin.

"They sure do look alike," I commented.

"They sure do. About the only real difference is the shipping weight—ours is heavier."

"Heavier?" I asked. "What makes yours heavier?"

"The Capo d'astro bar."

"What's a Capo d'astro bar?"

"Here, I'll show you. Get down on your knees."

Once under the piano he pointed to a metallic bar fixed across the harp and bearing down on the highest octaves. "It takes 50 years before the harp in the piano warps. That's when the Capo d'astro bar goes to work. It prevents that warping."

I left the National Sales Manager under his piano and dove under the Baldwin to find a Tinkertoy Capo d'astro bar at best. Same with Steinway.

"You mean the Capo d'astro bar really doesn't go to work for 50 years?" I asked.

"Well, there's got to be some reason why the Met uses it," he casually added.

I froze. "Are you telling me that the Metropolitan Opera House in New York City uses this piano?"

"Sure. And their Capo d'astro bar should be working by now."

Upstate New York looks nothing like the front of the Metropolitan Opera House where I met the legendary Carmen Rise Stevens. She was now in charge of moving the Metropolitan Opera House to the Lincoln Center.

Ms. Stevens told me, "About the only thing the Met is taking with them is their piano."

That quote was the headline of our first ad.

The result created a six year wait between order and delivery.

My point is this. No matter what the product or service, I promise you, the Capo d'astro bar is there.

(Keep in mind that this story was written more than 40 years ago, and Bud sounds like he's already in the Prima Donna Hall of Fame. They did things differently back then. Collaboration between the copywriter and art director, and between creatives and agency account people, wasn't as good as it is today. And attitudes about learning a client's business are also different.)

How intrepid a digger are you? How you answer that question will determine how you fill in this box on your creative brief.

Here are a few more questions to consider:
1. What did you do before?
2. How has it worked?
3. What led us to the need for this communication?
4. What's going on in the marketplace that could affect the work?
5. Who is our competition?
6. How do their products or services claims differ from ours?

8. What is the desired tone and mood?

Think of these choices as brand descriptors.

If you work with an established brand, you should already possess something called a "Brand Guideline," either a printed or online resource that gives you all aspects of the brand. That includes the official brand voice. Which should be the key words used to describe the brand. These brand descriptors should rarely change. They define the essence of your brand.

But you can spin them with each communication project. With practice, you'll become experts at using the appropriate descriptor or descriptors where they're truly appropriate. This will become part of your muscle memory.

And if you don't have a brand guideline?

Create one. Right away. Write your own guideline so everyone has a blueprint to follow.

When you get to the Brand Voice section, it will help to anthropomorphize the brand, asking "What is he or she like?" Keep your choices to no more than five words or phrases.

9. What are the deliverables?

Be careful with this one. I could have chosen a different way to ask, but I didn't.

I want to drive home a point: **Tell the creatives exactly what they're supposed to show you on the day they're supposed to show you something.** They need to know.

So if all you really want is concepts, ideas, unconnected to specific media like TV or DM, say so.

As in, "Deliver 3-5 unique concepts with heads and subheads."

If you want a full-blown campaign with multiple touch-points such as print, DM, outdoor and banner ads, say that.

And if you're not sure which avenue makes more sense—concepts only or concepts for specific media—meet with your creative director first and ask. Sometimes you'll get lots of helpful ideas by talking things over.

Remember, why should you take this on by yourself if you have options? Collaborate!

Sometimes you won't need to. You'll know that because the current (fill in the blank) has been running or in the mail or online for (fill in the blank) months, and you just need to refresh it. Same stuff, new creative. That's pretty clear.

Problems arise for creatives when they see a brief that asks for something specific when the option to discuss different approaches is open *but they didn't know that!*

Bring in your creatives early in the process to discuss deliverables. They have experience that can be invaluable to your communications plan. They're not going to recommend a TV campaign when what you need is a Web site. And if they do, shame on them.

On the other hand, if you really need an employee incentive program that requires a substantial rethinking of your entire communications plan, but you're insisting on three postcards, shame on you for not being open.

Your creative team has a lot of experience. Tap into it. And allow that option to be reflected in your creative brief.

What's missing from this brief?

Everything below finds its way onto a brief, and rightly so.

1. **Mandatories**
This category covers everything from logos, copyright information, toll-free telephone numbers and URLs, brand colors and brand standards.

2. **Timeline**
Translation: deadlines! Real and hoped for.

3. **Budget**
Sometimes this is a total spend, sometimes it's broken down by media. And sometimes it's just a concepting budget, meaning creative development. If it's the latter, best to discuss it during the briefing.

4. **Measurement strategy**
Clients are borrowing from direct-response advertising and expect more concrete ways to 1) measure how their dollars are spent and 2) track the open/read/click rate. Here's where you provide the details.

5. **Copy points**
Copy points should parallel communications objectives. If you have three or four communication objectives and 17 copy points, something is amiss. This is especially true on a print ad, but in a direct-mail package, a brochure or a press release, you may have more room to get into details.

99

6. **Brand position**

Usually, a brand position statement is something that was written long before the brief, so you should just pick it up from, say, a master brand brief.

7. **Call to action**

This is becoming more important for every piece of communication as clients expect their budgets to work harder. Every ad or TV spot or DM should ask the reader/viewer to do something. Clearly, succinctly, urgently.

8. **Offer**

Not every communication will have an offer. When it does, be sure to remember one key thing: the offer is never confused with the single-minded proposition. The SMP is the emotional connection to the product or service. The offer is the incentive to try it.

Creative Brief Sign-off.

Time to get started, right? Not so fast. Once the brief is done, you need to share it with key decision makers in your organization. These include but aren't necessarily limited to:

Your supervisor
Department head
Account Planner
Creative Director
Product Manager
Marketing Director

How your company functions will influence the role of the creative brief and who's responsible for reading it, and approving it with a signature.

Finally, the client for whom the brief was prepared needs to read it as well. And approve it.

Got all the signatures?

Now you can get started.

The finished document.

Creative Brief

1. What is the problem we're trying to solve?

Be clear: Sales are down and you need to acquire new customers. Your existing base is on the decline, so you need to do something to hold onto them. Your control package is working but it's time for a challenge. Tell the creative team what you're trying to fix or make better.

_____

_____

_____

2. Why are we communicating?

What are the two or three objectives you want the communication to make clear to readers? For example, to educate, romance, re-engage, motivate. Use verbs!

_____

_____

_____

3. What is the key emotional benefit?

Remember our Deep Target Dive. Choose one of the rational benefits from the proof above and ask the question: "Why is that important to you?" until you uncover the key emotional benefit.

_____

_____

_____

4. Who are we talking to?

Draw a word picture of the typical user. Be descriptive. Bring the target to life.

_____

_____

_____

5. What is the single-minded proposition (SMP)?

What's the one, most important thing you want to say about your product or service? Remember: one nail, not a bed of nails!

_____

_____

_____

6. What's the proof that the SMP is true?

List the most important benefits and why they're so important. Here's your chance to show how your brand or product is different from the competition's.

_____

_____

_____

7. What's the background?

Remember: he who digs deepest uncovers the treasure. What have you done before to communicate to these people? How has it worked?

_____

_____

_____

8. What is the desired tone and mood?

Choose no more than four or five characteristics to arrive at your tone.

_____

_____

_____

9. What are the deliverables?

Be general or be specific, such as "At least three concepts with headlines and subheads" or "One DM mail package with multiple OE snipes" or "One :30 and one :60 radio spot."

_____

_____

_____

"Can you see the

forest
for the **trees?**"

A truly inspired creative brief is usually, in fact often, accompanied by fireworks. You just know when you (or the writer) were in the zone and produced a brilliant document.

Even moderately well-written briefs reveal their inspiration.

And if you've been in the business for a while, you know a groaner when it comes out of the printer, or lands on your desk.

But what if you're not a veteran brief writer, copywriter or art director? What if you're brand new, or even just a couple years on the job?

Herewith are two tips that even the most seasoned brief writer or reader can use as a checklist against the high standards we all expect our creative briefs to achieve.

First, look carefully at the Single-Minded Proposition. Whatever it's called on your brief, start here. This is the one-sentence summary of what the entire creative brief has to say. So a reliable clue that your brief isn't aspiring to be inspiring will make itself known in this box.

Ask yourself: is the Proposition really single minded? Is it a paragraph of benefits? Or honestly and truly the most important benefit (singular)? Could you write it on the palm of your hand?

A few years ago I took a job as creative director at a marketing agency on a major international airline. My first day was about a week before a big presentation on a re-branding effort. So when I asked to see the creative brief, I was more than stunned when I read the Proposition. Essentially, it promised to save you money, let you get more work done en route, and give you better customer service.

It was the first triple-minded proposition I'd seen in a very long time. The creative team was so far into the process, and the client had insisted on it as it was written, that I had no choice but to play along.

If you ever come across a Proposition that tries to give you a laundry list of benefits, this is your first clue that the brief is not only *not* inspired, but that the brief writer is being lazy. I don't advise telling him that to his face. But I do believe you have the obligation to ask a few pointed questions so that you *both* arrive at one thing and one thing only.

107

Another clue that tells you you're having a bad day: when the language of the brief sounds more like it's meant to be read by a marketing manager or, worse, an accountant. I started noticing this trick — it's more like a cover up for not knowing what the heck to say — very early in my career. The brief writer drones on about how the creative you're being asked to produce is designed to... here comes the business language:

> **drive up sales**
> **lift quarterly profits**
> **reduce inventory**
> **expand market share**
> **respond to the competition**

This kind of drivel has no place on a creative brief. It ends up in the brief for two reasons:

First, because you aren't even trying to think like a creative, like someone who has to translate the brief into sales-driving concepts. You're engaged in *silo thinking*, as if you were an island separate from the creative team.

And second, because of silo thinking, there's no concept of collaboration with the creative team to write the creative brief. It's almost as if you've stepped into a time machine and transported back to pre-1960s, before the days of the Golden Age of advertising when the copywriter and the art director started teaming up and created a revolution in our profession.

108

So what can you do when you discover this kind of language in your own brief? Because I'm sure you didn't intend it, right?

Well, now's the time to ask a pertinent (no, I didn't mean impertinent) question:

Do these requests answer WIIFM?

That translates to:

What's in it for me?

If you can't answer that question, anything in the brief that doesn't answer it doesn't belong in the creative brief.

The well-written brief will tell the creative team what the ad has to say directly to the reader, directly to the user of the product or service.

If the brief focuses on what the ad is supposed to do *for* the product or the *bottom line* or the *quarterly report*, do yourself a favor and substitute "WIIFM-" related information instead.

Unless, of course, you don't mind an ad with a headline like this:

"We bring 97.8% of good things to life, which is 14% higher than we did last quarter."

Brief writers remember: the brief
helps the creative team unlock the "WIIFM" secret that needs to be communicated directly to the consumer. If you get lost in business lingo, your creatives will flounder. Think like a creative, talk to your creatives, collaborate, escape silo thinking and put your "consumer" hats on.

Avoid business jargon, lingo, marketing-speak, and bean-counting terms.

"It's
elementary
my dear Brief Writer!"

14 Let's do it backward.

Look at the creative first, then figure out the creative brief. I started using the technique before I learned where it originated. I uncovered it doing research on how they teach brief writing in the UK. Now you too can mimic the best.

This is a test of your deductive reasoning. What's the point? I want you to start looking a creative in new ways. Be more critical.

This exercise will help you when it comes to reviewing creative from your agency, creative department or freelancers. Your task is to take in each communication and think like a creative. Figure out what the one thing the communication is trying to impress upon you. What emotion is it trying to draw out of you?

If you can answer even just a few of the following questions, you should be able to figure out what the creative brief was. Much as I hate to say it—again—this isn't rocket science. Those of us who do advertising for a living have at least one thing on our side that others don't:

Lots of practice.

I'd probably win golf tournaments too if I had as much time to practice as Tiger Woods. Okay, that's a stretch. But you get the picture. Yes, you *do* get the picture.

So, find an ad, any ad. A TV spot, a piece of mail that's sitting in your inbox or waiting for you at home, listen to a radio spot on your commute. Flip through your favorite magazine or visit your regular web sites.

The point is, the sample creative is all around you. All you have to do is think critically about it rather than passively take in the message.

You can use your creative brief template, or rephrase the questions if you wish. Start here:

1. What does the advertiser want you to feel after you've seen the communication?

2. What is the single-minded proposition?

3. What's the proof that the SMP is true?

4. Can you figure out a key emotional benefit?

5. What problem is the communication trying to solve?

6. Who is the communication speaking to?

7. Can you figure out the tone of voice?

8. Did the communication work?

How did you do?

Practice this often and you'll discover that it gets easier. Your brief writing will improve too.

"Improvise, adapt, overcome."

Unofficial mantra of the Marine Corps

15 Briefing the creatives with your brief.

Remember the old joke: How do you get to Carnegie Hall?

No, you're not living a *Groundhog Day* nightmare. You've seen this page before. It's the same, only different.

When it's time to write a creative brief, you've come to the end of your strategic phase. The creative brief is the beginning of the creative phase.

So let's say you've completed writing your creative brief. Congratulations. Now what?

Like writing a brief, briefing your team is an art form. But there are a few rules of the road to assist you. First and foremost, practice, practice, practice.

Let's begin by identifying your pain and pleasure points.

What's the hardest part about briefing the creative team?

1.

2. _____

3. _____

4. _____

What's the easiest part about briefing creatives?

1. _____

2. _____

3. _____

4. _____

Some tips on briefing the beasts...er...creatives.

Let's begin with a list of dos and don'ts. And always remember who you're briefing! Whether you live in the fast-paced world of advertising, you work for an advertiser or an ad agency, even if you're in school and dream about working as a communications professional, time is rarely a luxury. But that's never an excuse for skipping a meaningful briefing session. If you've spent considerable time writing your brilliant brief, give it its due. Besides, if you don't your creatives will rebel.

Now I'm just gonna assume that you have a great relationship with your creatives. How could you not? They're lovable types. I'm also gonna assume that you *never* do the things I've listed on my "don't" list. But you'd think less of me if I didn't come right out and say them.

Creative briefing no-nos:

1. Slide your completed creative brief under the doors of the creative team and run for the hills.

I know, you'd never do this. You're good people. You're professional and all. Just thought I'd mention it in case, you know, you went temporarily insane. Or something.

2. Gather your creative team in the conference room, hand out the creative brief and then read it in a dull monotone—word for word—like it was yesterday's weather report.

Of course you'd never do that. I'm just saying.

3. Get up and leave after reading your brief in a dull monotone—word for word—like it was yesterday's weather report.

I know! I know! You've never done this.

4. Wait until five minutes before your scheduled briefing to prepare for your scheduled briefing.

What I said before.

5. Invite the client to sit in.

If you're on the client side, do yourself a favor. If this ever happens to you, politely decline. Why? Have you heard the joke about what you should never watch being made— sausages, and legislation? Well, let's add one more. A client participating in a creative briefing on his or her own product. If you've ever wondered what it would be like to walk in on a bunch of teenagers who've been talking about you, just try this.

6. Meet only once with your creative team for the briefing.

It's an ongoing conversation, not a speech. Consider yourself a successful briefer when your creative team comes back a day or two later and has more questions.

Summary

While these "no-nos" and some of the "dos" are almost self-apparent, it bears remarking that the entire point of a briefing is to engage. To collaborate. To put lots of heads together and go a little deeper. This is a team effort. No one has a monopoly on *clear thinking*. No one should put that much pressure on him or herself. That means you.

Creative briefing dos:

1. Make your briefing inspirational

Know your audience! You're talking to the creatives now. Not the product manager or the marketing guy. Especially not the accountant.

2. Speak in everyday language.

Please don't use marketing buzz words and business jargon. I can't give concrete examples because I don't know your industry or your client base, but you know them. Think about the last time you heard a physician interviewed on the nightly news who spoke as if everyone listening was also a physician. It's annoying. Creatives don't talk like this. You don't want your communications to either.

3. Show your team you've put some real thought into the briefing.

Remember, your job is to inspire your creative team. The amount of time and energy you devote to the effort will be rewarded. Bring the creative brief to life in your briefing. Creatives can be a jaded bunch. But they're intuitively very strategic in their thinking. Enliven your briefing by getting out of the office. Go where the brand lives. If it's a food product, blindfold the team and have them taste the client's and the competitors' brands. Insist on a factory, plant or facility tour. Get your hands on competitive communications and create a wall in a conference room where they can be read and studied.

4. Creative briefing is a conversation. Keep it going.

You didn't try to shove everything into the creative brief. Treat the briefing the same way. Let me repeat something from the "don't" list: Chances are you've done a successful briefing job when the team comes back with more questions. That's a good thing.

"A **leader**
without followers
is just someone **out for a**
stroll."

16 A call for transformation.

I'm also a regular blogger on the subject of the creative brief, and I invite you to visit, read a post here and there and weigh in when you feel like it. My blog is at

howardibach.com

I had the privilege of making a presentation to a Minneapolis marketing services agency not long ago and I came away with an inspiration, which became a post on my blog. I'm reproducing it here by way of a closing thought for creative brief writers everywhere. The post was entitled, "Alchemy is alive and well if you believe." Consider it a challenge:

The popular understanding of the word alchemy is the *transformation* from one substance, say stone, into another substance, usually gold.

I'd say that's a pretty darn good definition of what a creative brief can achieve.

It all depends on you, the brief writer.

How grand a promise does your brand make? Can it reach higher? Could it promise more?

How deep can you penetrate the heart of your brand's zealot? Or the heart of the one who's perched on the edge of trying it for the first time?

In my experience, the typical answer to these questions is, "I dunno, we'd need tons of research and the client doesn't want to spend the money."

Baloney.

I'm not belittling research. On the contrary. I'm challenging that kind of narrow thinking in the absence of a research budget. You may never get the research budget you want or need. But that can't and shouldn't stop you if you know how to make the most of the creative brief.

The brief isn't a box. It's a door with a sign on it reading, "I dare you to enter."

Just about every creative brief template I've read has all the right questions that can lead you and your team to bigger, more exciting *transformational* places for your brand. The question is, are you willing to take the time and energy to arrive at bigger, more exciting transformational *answers*?

Most briefs ask a question along these lines: "What is the single-minded message we want to communicate?"

What if you proposed this response:

"Brand X will let you live forever."

Riiiiiight. You can just see the product manager's face now, can't you?

Can you defend that statement? Can you substantiate it?

Hmm. Probably not.

But remember, you're working on the creative brief. This is the *I dare you* part.

My advice is to ask yourself, "Okay, so if I can't promise immortality, how close can I get to it and still have a believable brand message?"

I can't answer that one. You're the brief writer.

My mission is to open your eyes to the possibilities the brief gives you.

Your job is to take the dare.

And that, dear brief writer, is how you can compose
brilliant, inspired creative briefs from this day hence.

Go
forth and
dazzle.

Glossary

What follows should not be taken as gospel. It's my interpretation of these concepts after having been in the business for more than 20 years. We're not talking about an exact science here. There's a degree of subjectivity to these definitions.

Benefit

The advantage that you get from a particular feature of a product or service. For example, the feature could be...the built-in GPS device in your car. And the benefit is, you feel absolutely confident about navigating anywhere because you'll never get lost. You're a regular Daniel Boone explorer worthy of the National Geographic!

Brand

A car is a car. But Lexus is a brand. Why? Because you associate very specific emotions to that automobile when you own a Lexus. Even when you just think about owning a Lexus. These emotions establish a relationship between you and the brand.

As professional communicators, our job is to either create brands from scratch, an experience few of us actually get to do, or more likely to be brand guardians. That is, we go to work directly for a brand, such as Apple, or we work for a marketing services company, ad agency, PR firm or interactive company, and we work on specific communications assignments for well-known brands.

Brand position

This is the mental space that the brand is perceived to occupy in the mind of the target audience. I recommend the use of first person–I or we–when writing a brand position statement, to connect it directly to a consumer. For example, "When I'm on AOL and using the Internet I'm in a safe place."

Business objectives

These are the overall objectives for a business as a whole. These objectives lead to the strategies for the business and its various departments. They are usually about growing the business, increasing sales, hitting targets, beating goals, and things of this nature. All of which are or should be measurable, by the way.

Business objectives live a number of levels above marketing and communications objectives, which explains why they're not relevant for creatives to do their jobs effectively.

Call to action (CTA)

Language used to motivate an action by the reader or listener. Not to add any pressure, but if your CTA is wimpy, well, you get the picture. Be bold, be direct, be confident. A lot rests on these simple words.

Creative brief

Your road map. Your Sherpa. Your guide to the buried treasure. The creative brief is the contract between the client and its agency, and between the agency account team and the creative team. It spells out in inspiring terms exactly what needs to be produced to solve a specific business communication problem.

Demographics

The nuts and bolts of who your target is: specific characteristics such as age, gender, ethnic background, income, education, profession or work status, owner v. renter, geographic location.

Feature

These are the qualities unique to a product or service that distinguish it in the marketplace. Everything has features, from a potato chip to a rocket ship. Some are tangible, as in a rocket ship's, you know, rocket. Some are metaphorical, as in a potato chip's "it" factor—it's that "je ne sais quoi" quality.

Make a list of features. Lots of them. Be creative. You'll toss some, but that comes later. The more you can come up with, the more opportunities you have to assign benefits to them and find emotional hooks.

Marketing objectives

Marketing objectives are a level above communications objectives. They are important for the team to know and understand, but they're not vital from a creative execution point of view. They usually refer to measurable increases or improvements of awareness of a product or service.

In other words, if you want to sell more widgets, the creative team needs to know why the widget is desirable. The fact that Widget Inc. wants to increase its market share by next quarter doesn't help the creative team figure out how to do it.

Offer

A free or almost-free item or service that acts as an incentive for the target audience to try the product or service you're selling. But please, don't confuse the offer with the reason why you're selling the product or service in the first place.

130 "On brief"

Creative concepts that achieve the objectives of a well-written creative brief. Just remember, creatives work "from" a brief, not "to" a brief. The latter is restricting.

Persona

A complete biography of the target audience for a product or service, usually a combination of demographic and psychographic insights, plus information gleaned from a Deep Target Dive. The resulting snapshot gives you a well-rounded view of who you're appealing to.

Psychographics

The attributes that relate to personality, values, attitudes, interests or lifestyles of your target audience. They can also be referred to as IAO variables (Interests, Attitudes and Opinions). Combined with demographics, you have the makings of a persona.

Single-minded proposition (SMP)

Think of the best tag lines in advertising, and you get the idea. These precious words capture the essence of a product or service. More than any other part of the brief, this is the kicker. This one sentence or phrase is the brief. And it's a true artist who can assemble the words to make an elegant, definitive SMP. Master this part of the brief, and you will go far.

Substantiation or, "Show me the money!"

This is the proof, the quantifiable evidence, that your SMP is believable. Your knowledge of your product's or service's brand identity should kick in right about here. Go back to the brand and examine all the reasons why it's desirable, lovable, hugable—and here you will find the proof that your claim is valid.

Tactics

The strategy is the plan you devise to reach your objectives. The tactics are the specific actions you choose to achieve your strategy. For example, tactics are producing a meeting, creating a TV and print campaign, building a lease-retention program.

Tone of voice

This refers to the four or five specific words or phrases you choose to describe the tonality or mood you want the creative team to keep in mind when they develop the communications. For example, you could choose: Warm, humorous, urgent, sophisticated, insightful.

Tone of voice can change from communication to communication, and depends on the objectives of each project. For a sale or special promotion, you might want to emphasize urgency, whereas for a retention effort, warmth, friendliness and reassurance might be preferable.

Unique selling proposition

This can be synonymous with the single-minded proposition. I prefer to elevate this phrase to encapsulate the entire brand. It's a subtle distinction, and open to debate, but when you can use both to mean different things, you have more ammunition to define your projects. And consequently fewer opportunities to create misunderstandings and waste time and dollars.

Resources and references

Web sites

The Account Planning Group (United Kingdom):
www.apg.org.uk

Institute of Practitioners of Advertising (United Kingdom):
www.ipa.co.uk

Account Planning School of the Web:
russelldavies.typepad.com

Slideshare: www.slideshare.net

World Advertising Research Center (United Kingdom):
www.warc.com

Books

Bendinger, Bruce. *The Copy Workshop Workbook*. 3rd Edition. 2002. Print.

How To Plan Advertising. 2nd Ed. Ed. Alan Cooper. New York:Cassell, 1997. Print.

Steele, Jon. *Truth, Lies and Advertising: The Art of Account Planning*. New York:Wiley, 1998. Print.

Taylor, Alice Kavounas. *Strategic Thinking For Advertising Creatives*. London:Laurence King Publishing. 2014. Print.

Young, James Webb. *A Technique for Producing Ideas*, by James Webb Young. New York:NTC/ Contemporary Publishing Co., 1988. Print.

Articles

Brooks, David. "The New Humanism." *Nytimes.com. The New York Times.* May 11, 2011. Web. May 11, 2011.

Barker, David, "How to write an inspiring creative brief" *Admap Magazine*, July 2001, Issue 419. Print.

Diamond, Jeremy. "Come to the edge and fly ... How to create a brief that sets creativity free." *Viewpoint.* August 2002. Print.

Fleming, John H., Curt Coffman and James K. Harter, "Manage Your Human Sigma." *Harvard Business Review.* July-August 2005. 107-114. Print.

Henry, Steve. "How to write a great brief." *Admap Magazine.* November 1997. Print.

Shaw, John, and Sutherland, Rory. "True Crime, toolkits and the Big Ideal." *Market Leader.* Summer 2007, Issue 37. Print.

Southgate, David. "Three key steps to creative briefing." *World Advertising Research Center (WARC).* June 2009. Print.

White, Roderick. "Briefing creative agencies." *Admap Magazine.* January 2008. Print.

Recommended titles

Hitting the Sweet Spot: How Consumer Insights Can Inspire Better Marketing and Advertising, by Lisa Fortini-Campbell, 2001, Copy Workshop

Answer to questions about a feature and a benefit on page 77:

Your product is a one-million-dollar life insurance policy from MetLife.

What's the feature?
The $1,000,000 payout if you die. (There may be other features, but you're really buying a $1M policy for, um, the one-million dollars.)

What's the benefit?
Peace of mind that your family or loved one will be taken care of if you die.

Did you get it right?

About the Author

Howard Ibach is an author, essayist, adjunct college instructor, workshop facilitator and public speaker. In 2009, *How To Write An Inspired Creative Brief* was ranked #7 on About.com's "10 Advertising Books You Absolutely Must Read." It is now ranked #1. He is available to present both his one-hour conversation on the Single-minded Proposition, and Inspired Creative Brief Workshop, a one-day immersion seminar on the nuts and bolts of writing inspiring creative briefs. Please visit howardibach.com for more information.

Howard has worked at some of the top advertising agencies in the country, notably Hoffman York & Compton in Milwaukee; DDB Direct, Team One Advertising, Direct Partners, Brierley & Partners, Rubin Postare & Associates, OgilvyOne, Grey Direct West (now G2) and Wunderman in Los Angeles; and Carlson Marketing Group and Campbell Mithun in Minneapolis.

He lives in Los Angeles.

Good luck. And happy brief writing!

©2015 Howard Ibach

Write better briefs in one day.

Howard Ibach's **Inspired Creative Brief Workshop** will show you how to write better creative briefs in a step-by-step process. After his workshop, you will:

- Write tighter, clearer briefs
- Have a new vocabulary for writing creative briefs
- Review creative with more confidence
- Be more confident in directing and working with creative teams
- Be a brand wizard

Here's what others who have attended the workshop have to say:

The **Inspired Creative Brief Workshop** is designed for account and creative team members. It's a 6-hour, team-based interactive workshop that includes an 80+ page workbook, multiple thought exercises and opportunities to write briefs from scratch.

For more information, or to book a workshop, visit
www.howardibach.com today.

CPSIA information can be obtained at www.ICGtesting.com
Printed in the USA
BVOW03s0400180915

418240BV00010B/266/P